YOUR KNOWLEDGE HAS VALUE

- We will publish your bachelor's and master's thesis, essays and papers

- Your own eBook and book - sold worldwide in all relevant shops

- Earn money with each sale

Upload your text at www.GRIN.com and publish for free

Scientific Writing and APA Style. Distance Learning for Students

A Short Guide

Eirini Papachristou

Bibliographic information published by the German National Library:

The German National Library lists this publication in the National Bibliography; detailed bibliographic data are available on the Internet at http://dnb.dnb.de.

ISBN: 9783346275325
This book is also available as an ebook.

© GRIN Publishing GmbH
Nymphenburger Straße 86
80636 München

Print and binding: Books on Demand GmbH, Norderstedt, Germany
Printed on acid-free paper from responsible sources.

The present work has been carefully prepared. Nevertheless, authors and publishers do not incur liability for the correctness of information, notes, links and advice as well as any printing errors.

GRIN web shop: https://www.grin.com/document/943288

A Short Guide on Scientific Writing and APA Style for Distance Learning

Eirini D. Papachristou

Preface

This Guide includes the design and development of a printed educational material - suitable for distance learning - which refers to the writing of a good scientific paper and references with APA (American Psychological Association) style . *Part One:* The theoretical framework on which the Guide design was based is first described, namely: The importance of specially designed educational material in Distance Learning, the characteristics and principles of adult learning, and the particular characteristics of printed educational material in Distance Education. *Part Two:* The educational material is developed with the title of: "How do we prepare a good academic paper and how do we write references to the APA style - a guide to good practice for distance Education".

Eirini D. Papachristou

PART ONE
OPEN AND DISTANCE EDUCATION

1.1. Learning and teaching materials in Distance Education

Distance education is a method of education in which the student learns while away from his teacher, based on specially designed educational material and the quality of communication with the teacher. Educational material "is the main driver of the teaching process" (Lionarakis, 2001: 33) and should therefore satisfy two essential requirements:

➢ Be structured so that learners learn from it with as little help as possible from the teacher.

➢ Enable the student to choose the place, time and learning pace of his study (Matralis, 1998a: 48-49).

In order to meet these requirements, the educational material used in distance learning should perform the following functions (Matralis, 1998c:24):

o Guide the student through his study.

o Promote student interaction with learning materials.

o Explain difficult points and concepts.

o Evaluate and inform the student of his progress.

o To motivate and encourage him.

o Allow him to freely choose the location, time and pace of his study.

A good package of educational materials must, according to Rowntree (as cited in Matralis, 1998a, 1999: 55), to "...containing a teacher on standby. Once the student opens the package this teacher becomes active immediately and is ready to help him learn."

In distance learning printed material, despite the rapid development of new technologies, is the principal or sometimes unique form of educational material and includes: books and manuals, study guides, worksheets, maps, diagrams, photos, newspaper and magazine articles. The comparative advantages of printed material can be summarized as follows:

➢ It is familiar and acceptable to all trainees.

3

- It helps the student to determine the learning pace of his study.
- The distribution and receipt of the printed material by students does not require any planning or timetable.
- Provides easy "navigation" to its content.
- It can be easily used anywhere.
- Its development technology is widely known.
- It has low production costs.
- It is effective for transmission of large volume of material.
- It can be easily revised and corrected.

However the printed material has the following limitations:

a) Contains no sound and motion and

b) Makes it difficult to interact with the trainee (Matralis, 1998b: 28-30).

1.2. The characteristics and learning principles of adult learners

The design and development of educational material in Open and Distance Education should take into account the characteristics of adult learners, but also their basic learning principles. Adult trainees:

- They have specific needs and limited time.
- They have a large pool of experience.
- They have a shaped personality (Kokkos, 1998: 23-24).

The main learning principles which adults learn from are: (a) Thinking is related to action, (b) The focus of the educational process is on learners, (c) A broad path towards knowledge, (d) Critical thinking, (e) Interactive teacher - student relationships (Kokkos, 1998: 27-48).

1.3. The specific features of the educational material in Distance Education

During its evolutionary course, the printed educational material acquired the following special characteristics:

a) *Purpose:* Where the creator of the educational material makes a general statement of his intentions, briefly describing what will be presented in this piece of matter.

b) *Expected results:* they are a clear description of what the student will be able to do when he studies the capital (Matralis, 1998b: 53-54).

4

c) *Key Concepts:* They inform students of the basic concepts around which the content of the text they are studying revolves, and should be few in order to show the internal coherence of the text (Banou, 2001:66-67).

d) *Preliminary remarks:* They are placed immediately after the key concepts and present the content of the section, the intentions of the author, and mainly introduce the student into the internal logic of the text (Banou, 2001:67).

e) *Fragmented presentation of the material:* Helps students determine the pace of their study while encouraging them to continue their efforts (Matralis, 1998a: 39).

f) *Explanatory titles and subtitles:* help the student not to make the wrong choices in the selective reading that will probably follow (Matralis, 1998a: 43).

g) *Basic text:* it is the basic core of educational material. It stimulates students as it involves them in curing material, promoting both the interaction of students with educational material and the interaction of the parties between them (Lionarakis, 2001: 42-43).

h) *Study comments:* Provide specific instructions and advice directly related to the location (Matralis, 1998a:45).

i) *Tables and graphs:* are linguistic or semi-linguistic elements of educational material supporting and explaining the texts (Lionarakis, 2001: 47).

j) *Case examples and studies:* They are an important teaching tool as they help the student to gain insight into and better understanding of matter (Matralis, 1998a: 40).

k) *Self-assessment activities and exercises:* They help students to learn by making use of existing knowledge and to make extensive progress towards knowledge.

l) *Summary:* It is usually a small text that links the previous ones to the next, referring to the expected results (Banou, 2001: 68).

m) *Bibliography:* It gives the student an incentive to deepen matter and evaluate his learning course (Lionarakis, 2001).

n) *Guide for further study:* contains articles, books, audiovisual and/or electronic media proposed by the author to students to study in addition to printed educational material (Banou, 2001).

1.4. The stages of design and development of the specific printed educational material

In this case, a written study guide suitable for distance learning was designed, which refers to the writing of written work and how we use and write bibliographical references to the APA style. After the definition of the theoretical framework, the educational material design, which includes the following main stages (Matralis, 1998a), follows:

> ➢ *Study of the characteristics of the users of the material:* The following brochure is intended for students studying from a Distance, who are familiar with terms such as purpose, expected results, key concepts, introductory remarks, etc. However, as adults are concerned, it is necessary for the material to take advantage of their existing experiences and knowledge and to promote a broad approach to knowledge. It therefore contains activities, examples, parallel texts. In addition, due to the professional and family responsibilities of students, the material is designed to respect the pace of their study and to enhance their confidence by encouraging them to continue. This is why the material is divided into small sections with explanatory titles, summaries and frameworks for important topics.

> ➢ *Setting the intended teaching objectives*: The purpose of creating the printed material is to help students properly write their academic papers and use the APA style for bibliographic references and references. The expected results are that when students complete the material study they will be able to:

a. In terms of knowledge: indicate the rules for proper academic work, the structure it should have, the language appropriate, the specifications for the correct appearance of the work, and how to draw up references and references to the APA style.

b. At the skill level: To write their academic work according to the above rules and make satisfactory use of the APA style.

c. At the level of attitudes and perceptions: accept the need to comply with these rules, to avoid "plagiarism" and understand the usefulness of the APA style.

> ➢ *Specify the analytical contents:* to meet the objectives set.

➢ *Selecting the various types of material:* The design shall be for printed training material only.

➢ *Review of existing material:* For the writing of the specific printed material were used: 1) General instructions for the preparation of written work, 2) APA – reference list 3) Referencing in academic document (Kotzé, T., 2007).

How to prepare a good academic paper

and references according to APA style:

A Good Practice Guide for Distance Education

How to prepare a good academic paper and references according to APA style: A Good Practice Guide for Distance Education

Purpose

The purpose of this chapter is to help students studying from a Distance, to properly write their academic papers and to use the APA style for references.

Expected Results

Ending reading this chapter you will be able to:

- ☐ State the general rules for writing good academic papers.
- ☐ Describe the structure that every written work should have.
- ☐ Give examples of the most frequent errors in the language of the text.
- ☐ Layout the text page properly.
- ☐ Report the features of the APA style.
- ☐ Write bibliographic references with the APA style.

Key Concepts

- ➤ Text structure.
- ➤ Plagiarism.
- ➤ Text language.
- ➤ Bibliographical references.
- ➤ APA style.
- ➤ Appearance of written assignments

Introductory remarks

This chapter is divided into five sections. In the first section, we will present the general rules for good academic work, while in the second section we will refer to the structure of the text and the phenomenon of "plagiarism". In the third section we will talk about language and the most common grammar, syntax and typographical errors, and in the fourth section we will mention the specifications for the correct appearance of any academic work. Finally, in the fifth section we will present the main features of the APA style.

Unit 1.1

General rules for the preparation of written works

The preparation and evaluation of written work is an important component in a distance learning scheme. When writing your work focus on:

1. Understand and answer accurately to the issue you have been given

First read the title carefully and make sure you understand what it asks. Then take note of the key concepts that you think are relevant to the work title and write down some basic ideas about the topic. Immediately afterwards expand the concepts you entered and write a summary of the work.

2. Organize your paper structure

Remember that academic work usually consists of three main parts: Introduction, mainly subject and conclusions.

3. Develop the topic in your own words and on your plan

Provide your thoughts and arguments in a structured way using your own words and expressions.

Unit 1.2
Text structure

Each written work should include:

> **Introduction:** where you explain the matter in your own words and say how you structure the work, how you respond to its requests and what methodology you follow.

> **Main body of the paper:** where you will produce a detailed and synthetic text by developing in your own words the information you have from the teaching materials or other bibliographic sources.

> **Conclusions:** You need to write a summary here, where you will identify the key points of the work you have done.

> **Bibliographical references:** At the end you should present the bibliographic references you used in your paper.

Plagiarism

Every time you use someone else's words or ideas in your text you have to mention it, or else we're talking about the "plagiarism" phenomenon. Plagiarism is considered a serious breach of the terms of the academic community and consists of:

- In presenting someone's words and ideas as your own without mentioning the source.
- In copying another student's work and presenting it as yours.
- Copying and pasting information directly from an online source without paraphrasing or inserting quotation marks.
- Copying information from courses (guides, presentations, examination topics).

Parallel texts

More about university policy of plagiarism phenomenon can be found at the following address: http://www.ais.up.ac.za/plagiarism/policies.htm.

ACTIVITY 1 - CHAPTER 1

Now try to write a text (at least 350 words) into a cognitive object that is familiar to you, following the structure that any written work should have.

Unit 1.3

Text language

Always try to use simple and comprehensive speech, with no big sentences, arguing and scientifically substantiating your views. To avoid the most frequent grammar, syntax and typographical errors remember:

- Leave a space after punctuation
- Indicate paragraphs using a recess.
- Use comma: 1) to separate unconnected sentences or words, 2) after the Vocative and 3) to separate subsentences from master sentences.
- Do not use sentences more than 4-5 rows.
- Properly separate paragraphs.
- Avoid the use of first person.
- Precisely define the concepts of words and phrases.

ACTIVITY 2 - CHAPTER 1

Do you remember the most frequent grammar, syntax and typographical errors? Write them and compare your response to what is mentioned in the section above.

Appearance of written assignments

Unit 1.4

Requirements for a good appearance:
- Your text should be typed on A4 sheets of paper.
- Not to exceed the word limit.
- Number the pages of your work.

Configure the text page as follows:

Font:	Times New Roman
Font size:	12
Page margins:	Top: 2,54 cm.
	Bottom: 2,54 cm.
	Left: 3,17 cm.
	Right: 3,17 cm.
Line spacing:	Double
Page numbering:	*Header*-right

Unit 1.5
APA Style

The APA style for the writing of scientific work is used in many of the social sciences and contains rules concerning the content and structure of the text, the writing mode, bibliographical references and generally the preparation of a scientific article for publication. Its main characteristic is that it divides the scientific text into modules, which allows the author to be creative and clearly illustrate his thoughts. But that also makes it easier for the reader to find the information he wants easily.

Writing references citations and reference list - APA style in a scientific paper

- APA style uses the author/date method of citation in which the author's last name and the year of the publication are inserted in the actual text of the paper.
- If the quotation is longer than forty words, it is set off without quotations marks in an indented block (double spaced). The source is cited in parentheses after the final period
- If citing a work discussed in a secondary source, name the original work and give a citation for the secondary source. The reference list should contain the secondary source, not the unread primary source.

Reference list can be found at the end of a scientific paper in a separate page in alphabetical, non-numbered order. Each reference should include the following – Examples from www.apastyle.org:

- ✓ **Books:** Sapolsky, R. M. (2017). *Behave: The biology of humans at our best and worst.* Penguin Books
- ✓ **Articles:** Grady, J. S., Her, M., Moreno, G., Perez, C., & Yelinek, J. (2019). Emotions in storybooks: A comparison of storybooks that represent ethnic and racial groups in the United States. *Psychology of Popular Media Culture, 8*(3), 207–217

Parallel texts

See more in 7th Edition - Publication Manual of the American Psychological Association APA online: http://www.apastyle.org

Chapter summary

In this chapter:

> ➢ We have mentioned the general rules for the writing of α good scientific paper.

> ➢ We have talked about the phenomenon of 'plagiarism', which is a very serious violation of the terms of the academic community.

> ➢ We have reported the most frequent grammatical, editorial and typographical errors.

> ➢ We have set the standards for the proper presentation of the scientific work.

> ➢ We talked about the APA system and how to write reference citations and reference list.

References

APA Style (American Psychological Association. Available online
https://apastyle.apa.org/

Kotzé, T. (2007). *Referencing in Academic Documents.* 3rd edition. University of
Pretoria. Online: http//www.odl.gr

Kokkos, A. (1998). "Principles of Adult Learning". In: Kokkos, A. & Lionarakis, A.,
Open and Distance Education – Teacher-student relationships, Ed.: A.,
Kokkos, Lionarakis, A. & Matralis, X. Volume B΄, Patra: Open Hellenic
University. (In Greek).

Lionarakis, A. (2001). "Open and Distance multiform education. Concerns for a
qualitative approach to the design of teaching materials". In: *Views and
concerns about the open and distance education.* Ed.: A. Lionarakis. Athens:
Propobos. (In Greek).

Matralis, X. (1998a). "Existence-Design of specific training material". In: Bergidis,
D., Lionarakis, A., Lykourgiotis, A., Makrakis, B. & Matralis, X. (1998).
Open and Distance Education – Institutions and Functions, Ed.: A. Kokkos,
Lionarakis, A. & Matralis, X. *Volume A,* Patra: Open Hellenic University. (In
Greek).

Matralis, X. (1998b). «Purpose and expected results». In: Kokkos, A., Lionarakis, A.,
Matralis, A. & Panagiotakopoulos, X. Open and Distance Education-
Educational material and New Technologies, Ed.: A. Kokkos, Lionarakis, A.
& Matralis, X. *Volume C,* Patra: Open Hellenic University. (In Greek).

Matralis, X. (1998c). «Printed material in Distance Education». In: Kokkos, A.,
Lionarakis, A., Matralis, A. & Panagiotakopoulos, X. Open and Distance
Education-*Educational material and New Technologies,* Ed.: A. Kokkos,
Lionarakis, A. & Matralis, X. *Volume C,* Patra: Open Hellenic University. (In
Greek).

Banou, A. (2001). "Open and Distance Education. Issues of terminology and
methodology". In: *Views and Concerns on Open and Distance Education.* Ed.:
A. Lionarakis. Athens: Propobos. (In Greek).

YOUR KNOWLEDGE HAS VALUE

- We will publish your bachelor's and master's thesis, essays and papers

- Your own eBook and book - sold worldwide in all relevant shops

- Earn money with each sale

Upload your text at www.GRIN.com
and publish for free